The Wonder of Outer Space

Connie Jankowski

Earth and Space Science Readers:
The Wonder of Outer Space

Publishing Credits

Editorial Director
Dona Herweck Rice

Associate Editor
Joshua BishopRoby

Editor-in-Chief
Sharon Coan, M.S.Ed.

Creative Director
Lee Aucoin

Illustration Manager
Timothy J. Bradley

Publisher
Rachelle Cracchiolo, M.S.Ed.

Science Contributor
Sally Ride Science

Science Consultants
Nancy McKeown
Planetary Geologist
William B. Rice,
Engineering Geologist

Teacher Created Materials
5301 Oceanus Drive
Huntington Beach, CA 92649-1030
http://www.tcmpub.com

ISBN 978-0-7439-0563-3

Table of Contents

Outer Space

Have you ever stopped to gaze at the stars? Have you ever wondered if there might be life on other planets? Have you ever thought about how the **universe** began? If you answered "yes" to any of these questions, you are not alone!

Since the dawn of history, humans have always looked to the heavens with curiosity. That's why **astronomy**—the study of **planets**, stars, and **galaxies**—is thought to be the oldest science.

Astronomers are scientists who study space. Long ago, astronomers thought that the Earth was the center of the universe. They thought all the other planets and stars

An astronomer uses a telescope to view objects in space.

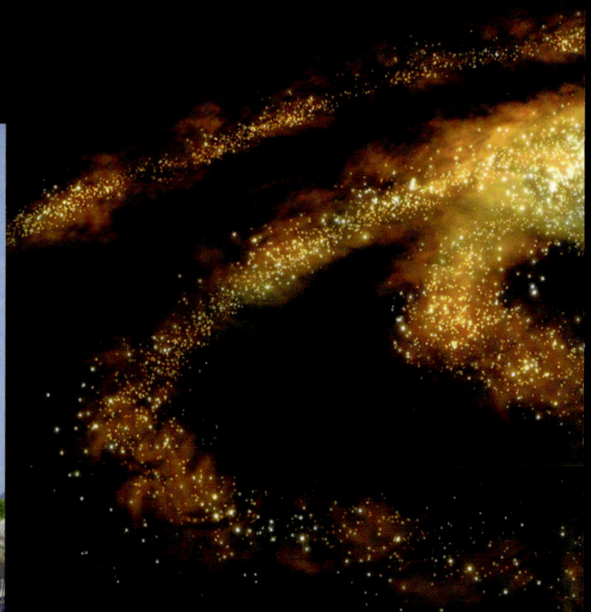

revolve around Earth. Now we know that Earth is only a tiny part of the universe. It is just one of eight planets in our **solar system**. Our solar system is just a tiny part of our **galaxy**, which is called the **Milky Way**. Outer space is made up of billions of galaxies and trillions of stars!

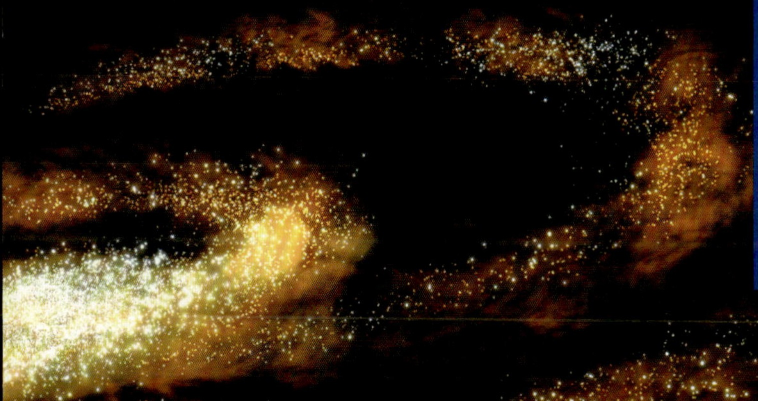

Still Growing

How big is outer space? No one knows for sure. Five hundred years ago it was thought to be only a little bit bigger than Earth. Scientists now know it is much bigger than anyone could have imagined. Using modern technology, they have learned that the universe is still growing outward in every direction.

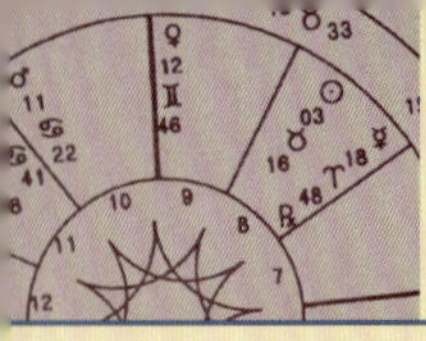

Early History

People have always been fascinated by space. In ancient times, people began to notice patterns in the sky. They saw that heavenly bodies appear to move in a regular manner. They saw the sun rise in the east and set in the west. As the sky grew dark, they saw tiny points of light appear. Most of these lights were stars. The ones that seemed to wander were planets.

These movements in the sky helped people keep track of time. They helped travelers find their way. They even helped farmers figure out when to plant and harvest their crops. People began to write down what they saw. Astronomy was born.

Of course, early astronomers had no idea that space existed much farther than the eye could see. Around 450 B.C., Greek astronomers started using math to study the motions of the planets and measure the size of the earth, sun, and moon.

an ancient Egyptian astronomer

Astrology or Astronomy?

Some ancient cultures believed that the positions of stars and planets were signs of what was going to happen on Earth. They used them to predict wars, good fortune, births, and even death. This system of belief is called **astrology**. Many people confuse astronomy with astrology. They are very different. Few scientists still believe in astrology. However, they have found that some ancient astrologers were good at tracking the motions and positions of stars and planets.

The twelve signs of the zodiac formed the basis of astrology and, to some degree, astronomy.

This satellite galaxy image is based on Big Bang radiation.

The Big Bang

The universe is a huge space that holds everything that exists, from the smallest grain of sand to the biggest galaxy. One of the biggest questions humans have long asked is, "How did the universe begin?"

Most scientists think the universe began with something called the **Big Bang**. The Big Bang theory says that about 13.7 billion years ago, the universe snapped into being. It started very small, but right from the start it was growing bigger. **Matter** spread out from the Big Bang to form stars, planets, and everything else in the universe.

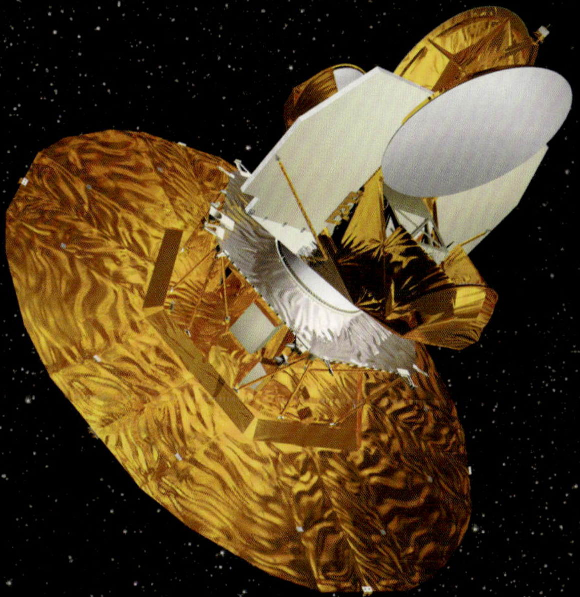

WMAP is a NASA probe that measures the leftover heat from the Big Bang.

Space continues to expand today. It appears to be slowing down, though. Gravity pulls matter together. It might be pulling the whole universe back together. Scientists are not sure if the universe will stop or keep expanding forever. Some think that one day, gravity will win and the universe will start to collapse on itself.

A Message From the Past

Did you know that static on your television may be caused by the Big Bang? Scientists say low levels of microwaves found in space are from radiation caused by the Big Bang!

Why Should We Explore Space?

Humans have always had a need to explore and learn from their surroundings. Understanding how the universe began and learning whether there might be life on other planets are two reasons why we study outer space. Astronomy also has changed our lives here on Earth.

Space travel has helped us in the fields of medicine, computer science, and the environment. Studying how an astronaut's body changes in space has helped treat diseases here on Earth. Being able to watch our planet from space has taught us about how pollution is hurting our environment. Our space program might help fix some of these problems in the future.

The space shuttle fleet has flown over 100 missions into space.

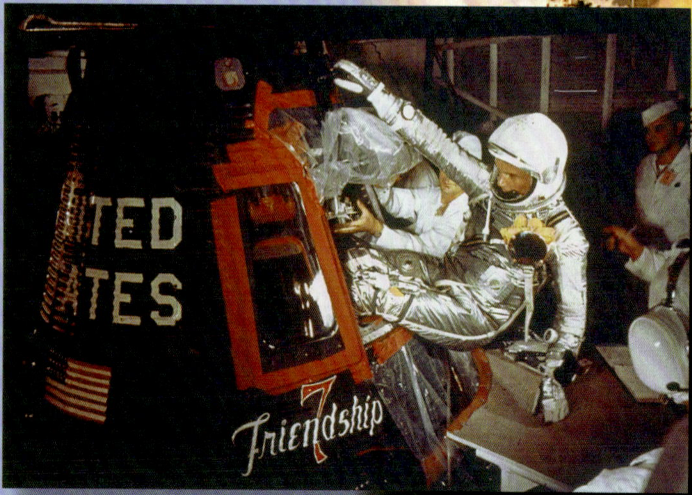

John Glenn boards his capsule *Friendship* 7. He was the first American in orbit.

Seeing the Future

When you listen to the weather report, do you ever wonder where that information comes from? **Satellites** sent into space are used to study the weather here on Earth. Satellites circle the planet and send back signals and photos. They are able to measure things like the wind speed inside clouds. These signals help us to predict the weather. They allow scientists to track hurricanes and other storms. This gives people a chance to prepare before a big storm hits. Many lives have been saved by the information provided by satellites.

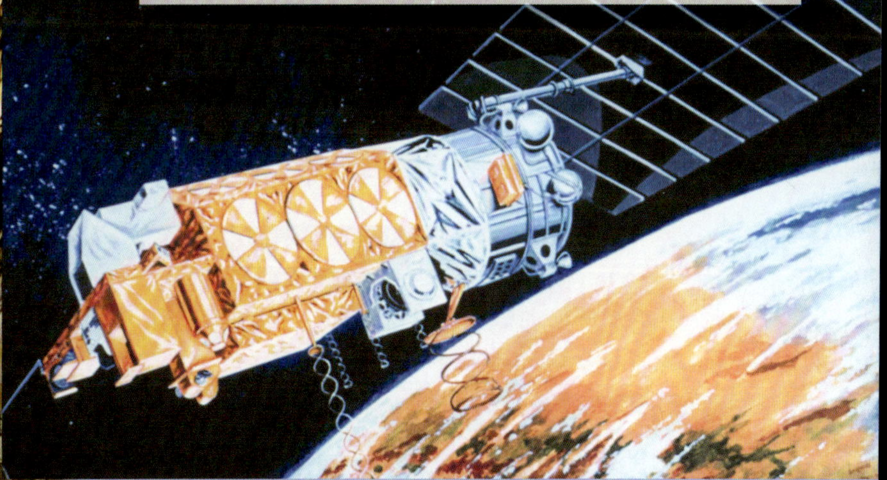

Satellites may one day gather solar power for use on Earth.

Journey to Space

The space age began in 1957 when the Soviet Union launched *Sputnik 1*. This was the world's first man-made satellite. Four years later, Soviet **cosmonaut** Yuri Gagarin became the first person to pilot a spacecraft.

Today, the largest space research group is the U.S. National Aeronautics and Space Administration (**NASA**). Its *Apollo 11* mission made the United States the first country to put a person on the moon. In 1969, astronaut Neil Armstrong became the first person to walk on the moon. His first words there are famous. He said, "One small step for man, one giant leap for mankind."

NASA later developed the **space shuttle**. This is a spacecraft that can be used over and over. Since 1981, the space shuttle fleet has

Russian cosmonaut Yuri Gagarin

had more than 100 successful flights. Sadly, two crews have been lost through tragic accidents.

In 1983, the **space probe** *Pioneer 10* became the first man-made object to leave the solar system. It was launched 11 years earlier!

From Fiction to Fact!

On television shows such as *CSI: Crime Scene Investigation*, on-screen detectives rely on science to solve crimes. NASA has been working on technology to give real-life crime fighters the tools they need. Scientists at NASA's Kennedy Space Center created a device to study the space shuttle after it was in a hailstorm. Lasers helped them figure out the scale of the damage. Detectives can now use this device to study crime scenes.

In 1969, Neil Armstrong became the first person to walk on the moon.

Why do we send people and equipment into space? Each mission starts with goals in mind. There are two kinds of missions: **manned** and **unmanned**.

Manned missions carry people into space. The astronauts on board perform experiments while in space. More than 400 astronauts have gone into space. Most manned missions stay within Earth's **orbit**.

Unmanned missions use remote-controlled spacecraft. Why would anyone launch a spacecraft without people on board? Some missions are unmanned when the risks are too great for people. Other unmanned missions include satellites that orbit the Earth for years. Some satellites are used for

The International Space Station uses unmanned vehicles like the one above to bring the astronauts necessary supplies.

communication and navigation. Space probes leave Earth's orbit and never come back. They study faraway planets, stars, and atmospheres.

Some missions go to places so far away that people could not survive the trip. We have sent unmanned probes to Mars, Venus, Jupiter, Saturn, Uranus, Neptune, Mercury, and Pluto. We know that these planets and **dwarf planet** do not support life. So, unmanned craft let us explore from afar!

Mission Control keeps track of both manned and unmanned missions.

Meet an Astronaut

Dr. Ellen Ochoa is a NASA astronaut. She was born in Los Angeles in 1958. She has been on four space flights and logged nearly 1000 hours in space! She is also an inventor with three patents. Ochoa is just one of many NASA scientists and astronauts working today.

First Woman in Space

The first woman in space was Soviet Valentina Tereshkova. She was on the spacecraft *Vostok 6* that launched in 1963. It orbited Earth 48 times in 71 hours!

Our Base in Space

Did you know there is a laboratory floating in outer space? In fact, it is one of the brightest objects in the night sky. It's called the International Space Station (ISS). It is like a home in space. Astronauts live there and carry out experiments. Sixteen nations have worked together on this project.

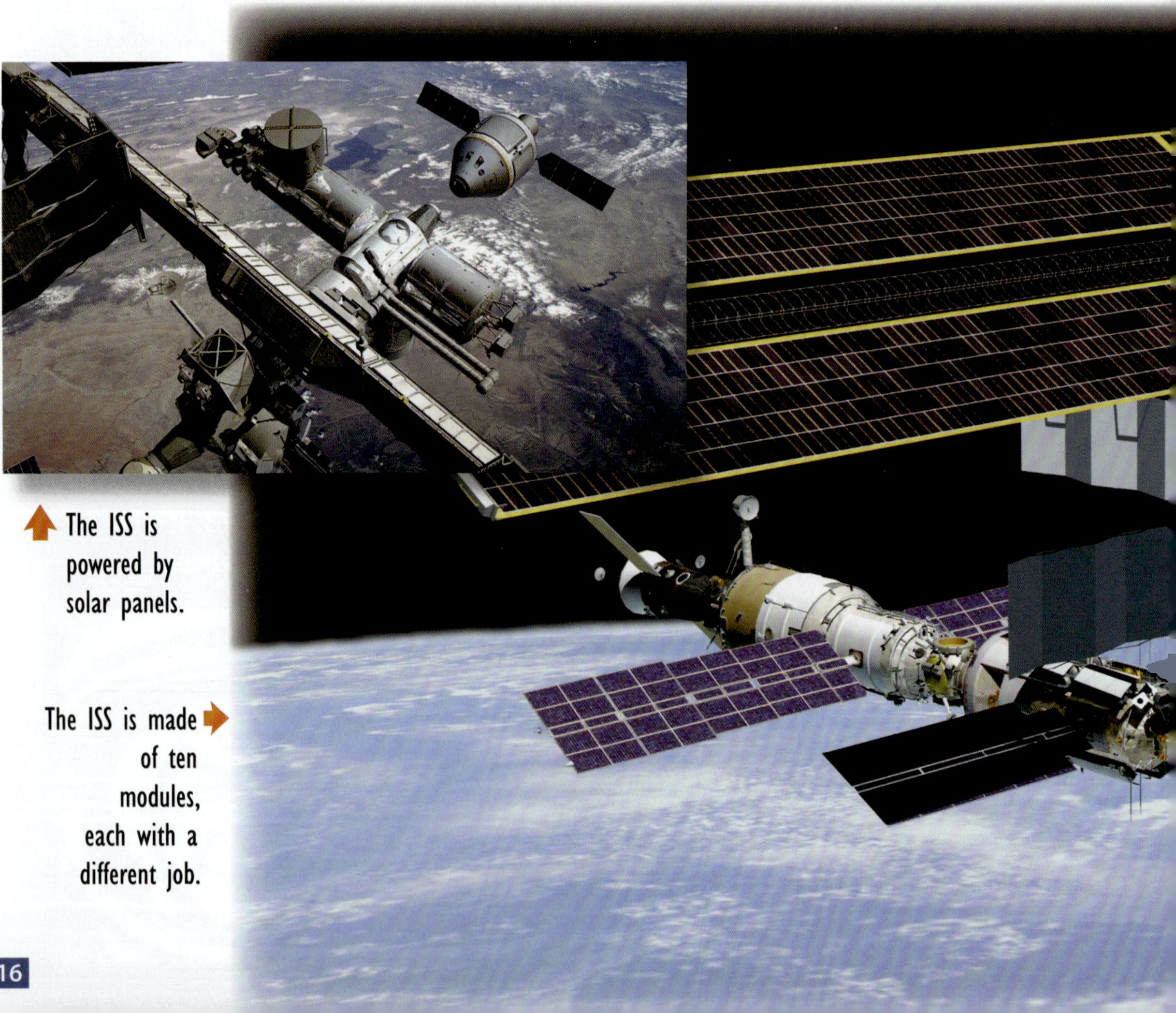

The ISS is powered by solar panels.

The ISS is made of ten modules, each with a different job.

There have been at least two people on board the ISS since the first crew arrived in 2000. Most crew members stay about six months. They do experiments that can only be done in space. They observe the universe from outside the **atmosphere**. Of course, land-based scientists are always in support of the ISS crew. They monitor their health and help with experiments. One day, the ISS may serve as a launch pad for missions to other planets such as Mars.

A Vacation That's Out of This World

In 2005, American Gregory Olsen took a vacation he won't soon forget. The wealthy scientist paid $20 million for a ride on a Russian space capsule to the International Space Station. He became the third space tourist to visit the International Space Station.

The Dangers of Space

Space is a dangerous place for humans for many reasons. There is no oxygen, so we can't breathe. In the shadow of a planet, temperatures are so low we would freeze. In direct sunlight, we would fry in the sun's heat.

Space suits let astronauts take their environment with them to space! These bulky suits protect them from the lack of oxygen and extreme heat and cold. Their spacecraft also protects them from **cosmic rays** and other forms of radiation.

Inside the spacecraft, special clothing is not needed once the astronauts reach orbit. The atmosphere in the spacecraft can be controlled. Astronauts must put on their space suits if they want to work outside of the spacecraft. Otherwise, they would have nothing to breathe!

When an astronaut works outside the safe environment of the space shuttle, it is called a spacewalk.

NASA space suits are called EMUs, or Extravehicular Mobility Units.

Space Food

Astronauts have a full menu from which to choose. They can eat fruit and crackers. They can heat water and cook pasta. They can have cookies for dessert. Astronauts have an oven to heat the food, but there are no refrigerators in space. The food is freeze-dried instead. And salt and pepper can only be used in a liquid form. Astronauts can't sprinkle regular salt and pepper on their food. The spices would float away! That is because there is no gravity within the space station.

The Great Observatories

Observatories have very powerful telescopes. They give an amazing view of the heavens from Earth. But there are clouds of gas and dust in Earth's atmosphere. They can block our view. So NASA launched telescopes into space. They allow us to get a much better look.

These orbiting telescopes are part of NASA's **Great Observatories** program. They take and send back to us pictures of planets, stars, and even Earth. Scientists can study outer space without leaving home!

The Chandra X-ray Observatory was packed up like this for its trip into orbit aboard a space shuttle.

This image of NGC 6751, also known as the Glowing Eye Nebula, was taken by the Hubble Space Telescope.

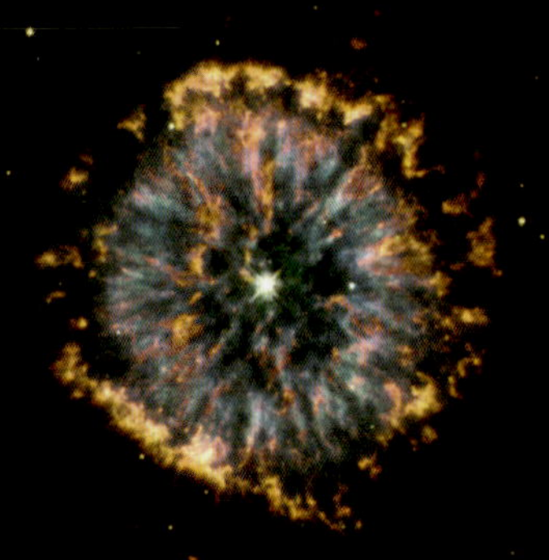

Floating Telescopes

The **Compton Gamma Ray Observatory** was the second telescope sent into space. It was launched from the space shuttle *Atlantis* in 1991. It weighs 17 tons! It has already completed its mission. It came down in the Pacific Ocean in 2000.

The third member of the Great Observatory family is the Chandra X-ray Observatory. This telescope is observing things like **black holes** in space. The mirrors on Chandra are the largest and smoothest mirrors ever built.

Hubble Space Telescope

the Compton Gamma Ray Observatory

The Hubble Space Telescope was the first of the four telescopes NASA sent into space. It is also probably the best known. It was launched in 1990. It orbits Earth more than 600 kilometers (nearly 400 miles) above its surface. Scientists on the ground control it. The pictures it has sent have helped them understand many things. They are learning about star birth, star death, and even how the galaxy was formed. Its images help scientists answer questions about how the universe began.

NASA's Spitzer Space Telescope is the fourth and final piece in NASA's Great Observatories program. It was launched in 2003.

The Spitzer Space Telescope senses **infrared light**. This helps astronomers see through clouds of dust in space. It is helping scientists find very young stars and new solar systems.

Milky Way image taken by the Spitzer Space Telescope

Spitzer Space Telescope

Aglow with Dust

Our galaxy, the Milky Way, is a dusty place. It is so dusty, in fact, that we cannot see its center with normal light. The Spitzer Space Telescope has helped astronomers cut through the clouds of dust. With it, we can see over 30 million stars in the inner part of our galaxy.

Spitzer is the largest infrared telescope ever launched into space. It is named for the first scientist to suggest placing telescopes in space. These telescopes have led to new discoveries about our universe.

Stargazing on the Islands

Most people know that Hawaii is a great place to sightsee. It is also one of the best places to watch the stars!

Many of the world's best observatories on land are in Hawaii. You can probably find an observatory near you, too. You can also visit one online.

What makes Hawaii good for stargazing? The dry and still air gives a clear view. The high altitudes and thousands of miles of ocean help as well. With few city lights around, the skies are nice and dark.

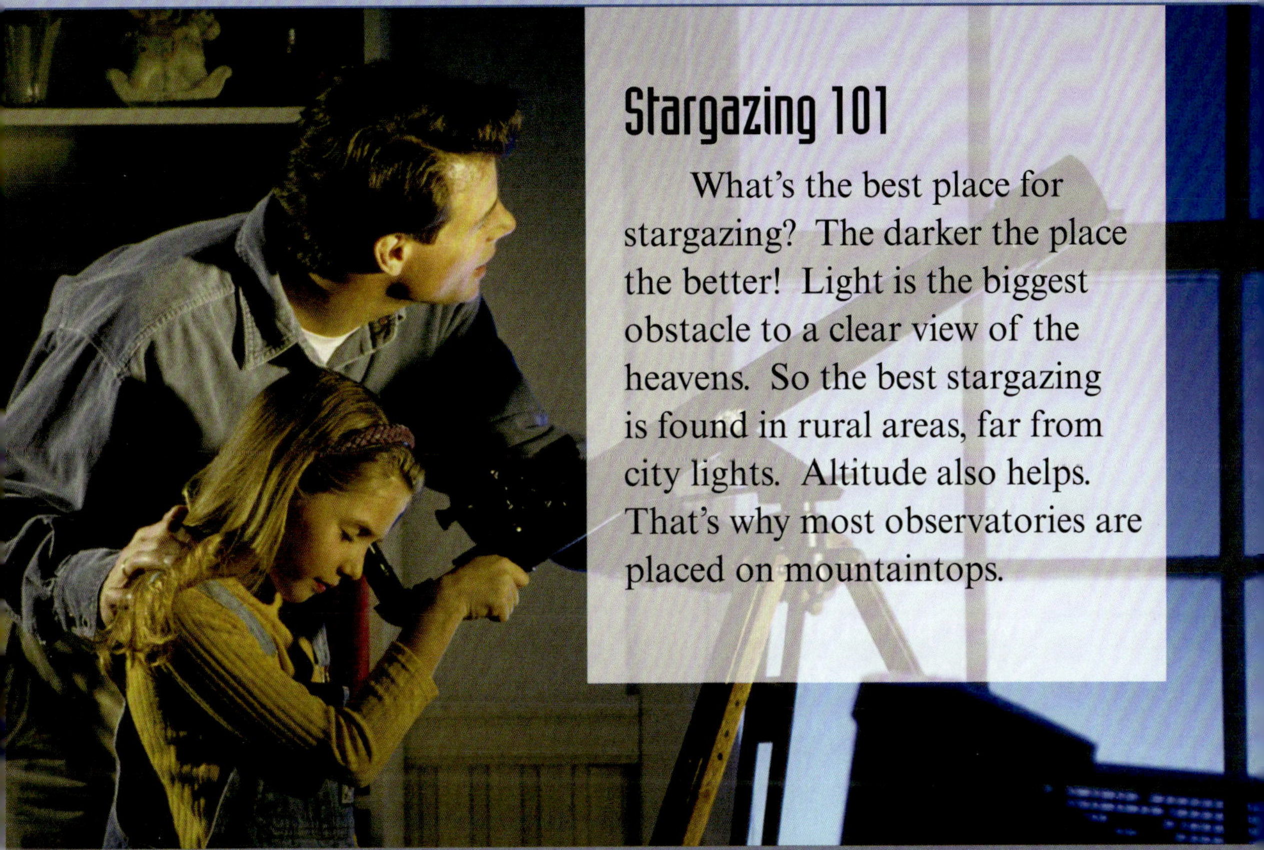

Stargazing 101

What's the best place for stargazing? The darker the place the better! Light is the biggest obstacle to a clear view of the heavens. So the best stargazing is found in rural areas, far from city lights. Altitude also helps. That's why most observatories are placed on mountaintops.

The Keck Twin Telescopes were built on Mauna Kea in Hawaii. From the top of this volcano, scientists watch the skies. They can see into the deepest parts of the universe. Each "twin" is eight stories high. It weighs about 300 tons. Mauna Kea is an inactive volcano. It does not erupt. So, it makes a good, high spot for an observatory.

The Keck Twin Telescopes are located on Mauna Kea on the island of Hawaii.

What's Next?

What does the future hold for space exploration? NASA's plans for the future will take us to new heights!

The next manned trip to the moon is planned for 2018. This mission will last about seven days. Scientists want astronauts to be able to produce water, fuel, and other necessities for life. Can homes on the moon be far behind?

There are also plans for astronauts to visit Mars by 2028. This would be a much longer mission. Astronauts could be on the planet's surface for 500 days!

Pluto should be getting a visit from Earth, too. Pluto is a dwarf planet at the edge of the solar system. In January 2006, NASA's *New Horizons* spacecraft began the very long journey to the dwarf planet. It will reach Pluto in 2015. The unmanned spacecraft will fly by Pluto and send images and data to Earth. *New Horizons* may uncover surprises that will help us learn more about our solar system and our universe.

NASA's Project Constellation plans to build a base on the moon as a stepping stone for a manned expedition to Mars.

Farms on Mars?

How can NASA keep a whole crew of busy astronauts healthy and well-fed for the two years that it will take to travel to Mars and back? Scientists are figuring out how to grow crops such as potatoes and peanuts in special greenhouses.

Lab: Mini Constellation Viewer

Constellations are patterns formed by stars. Centuries ago, humans used their imaginations to link star patterns. They did this by drawing dot-to-dot pictures in their heads. They named the constellations after ancient gods, objects, and animals. After you do this activity, try to find some constellations in the night sky.

Materials

- 35mm film canisters (one for each constellation you want to view) or other such containers
- scissors
- tape
- pushpin
- constellation patterns (page 29)
- paper
- pen

Procedure

1 Choose a constellation from the patterns on page 29. Trace it and cut it out on the dotted lines. (If you have a copy machine, you can copy it in that way.)

2 Tape the pattern in place over the bottom of the film canister.

3 Using a pushpin, punch a small hole through the paper and the canister for each star in the pattern.

4 Hold the film canister up to the light. You should see light through each hole.

5 Take the pattern off the canister. Trade with a partner and see if you can both figure out which constellation the other chose.

6 Try to find the same constellations in the night sky.

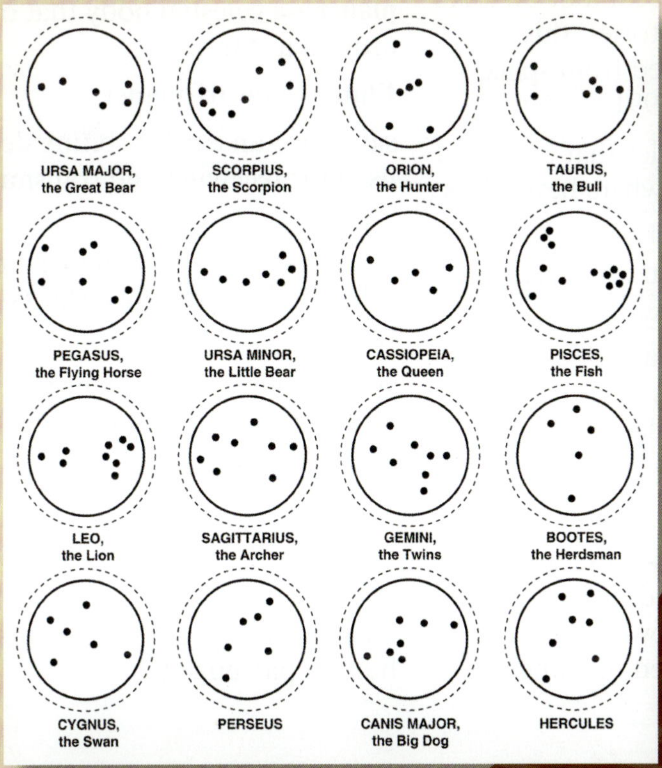

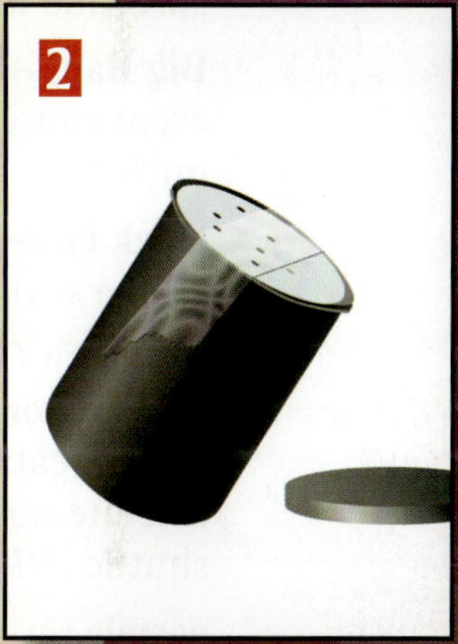

Glossary

astrology—belief that the position of stars and planets have an influence on human affairs

astronomer—a person who studies celestial objects

astronomy—the study of the universe and of objects in space such as the moon, the sun, planets, and stars

atmosphere—a layer of gases that surround a planet or moon

Big Bang—theory that a sudden event caused the beginning of the universe

black hole—invisible region in space with a strong gravitational field

Compton Gamma Ray Observatory—the second of NASA's four Great Observatories; this satellite was launched from space shuttle *Atlantis* in 1991

cosmic rays—particles that bombard the Earth from anywhere beyond its atmosphere

cosmonaut—Russian astronaut

dwarf planet—a celestial sphere that orbits the sun but has not cleared the neighborhood of its orbit of other bodies and is not a satellite

galaxy—a cluster of millions of stars bound together by gravity

Great Observatories—a series of four satellites created by NASA; all four are large, powerful space-based telescopes used to gather information

infrared light—electromagnetic radiation with wavelengths longer than visible light but shorter than radio waves

manned—space travel that includes human passengers

matter—anything that occupies space and has mass

Milky Way—the spiral galaxy in which our solar system exists

NASA—the largest public space-research program in the U.S.

observatory—place where you can use strong telescopes to view space

orbit—the path that a planet, moon, or celestial body follows around another body

planet—a celestial body that orbits around a star

Pluto—a dwarf planet

satellite—an earth-orbiting device used for receiving and transmitting signals

solar system—a system of planets or other bodies orbiting a star (such as the sun)

space probe—an unmanned craft sent into space to do research

space shuttle—a reusable U.S. spacecraft

universe—everything that exists anywhere

unmanned—space travel without human passengers

Index

Sally Ride Science

Sally Ride Science™ is an innovative content company dedicated to fueling young people's interests in science. Our publications and programs provide opportunities for students and teachers to explore the captivating world of science—from astrobiology to zoology. We bring science to life and show young people that science is creative, collaborative, fascinating, and fun.

Image Credits

Cover: NASA; p.3 R. Hurt/NASA; p.4 (top) Robert J. Beyers II/Shutterstock; p.4 (bottom) Photos.com; p.4–5 NASA; p.5 Jurgen Ziewe/Shutterstock; p.6 (top) Ingrid E. Stamatson/Shutterstock; p.6–7 (bottom) Stelian Ion/Shutterstock; p.6–7 North Wind Picture Archives/Alamy; p.7 Simon Detjen Schmidt/Shutterstock; p.8 NASA; p.8–9 Public Domain; p.9 Kerry Garvey/Shutterstock; p.10 (top) NASA; p.10 (bottom) NASA; p.10–11 NASA; p.11 NOAA; p.12 (top) NASA; p.12 (bottom) POPPERFOTO/Alamy; p.12–13 NASA; p. 14 (top) NASA; p.14 (bottom) NASA; p.15 (left) NASA; p.15 (right) NASA; p.15 (bottom) Bettmann/CORBIS; p.16 Reuters/CORBIS; p.16–17 NASA; p.17 DENIS SINYAKOV/AFP/Getty Images; p.18 (top) NASA; p.18 (bottom) Brand X/SuperStock; p.19 (top) NASA; p.19 (bottom) NASA; p.20 (top) NASA; p. 20 (left) NASA; p. 20 (right) NASA ; p. 21 (left) Trip/Alamy; p. 21 (right) Reuters/CORBIS; p.22 (top) NASA; p.22–23 NASA; p.23 (top) NASA; p.23 (bottom) NASA; p.24 NASA; p.25 (top) Photos.com; p.25 (bottom) W.M. Keck Observatory; p.26 (top) Jan Kaliciak/Shutterstock; p.26–27 NASA; p.27 (bottom) NASA; p.27 (right) NASA; p.28 (top) NASA; p.28–29 Nicoll Rager Fuller; p.32 Getty Images